KERE KERE YA

Orisha Coloring Book

Written and Illustrated by Oba Olff for Omidina Productions

Edited by Nirvanda Simm-Smith

Books. Content. Culture
www.Omidina.com

2020 All Rights Reserved

Copyright in progress © 2020 Oba Ade Dayo

All rights reserved. No part of this publication may be reproduced, distributed, or transmitted in any form or by any means, including photocopying, recording, or other electronic or mechanical methods, without the prior written permission of the publisher, except in the case of brief quotations embodied in critical reviews and certain other non commercial uses permitted by copyright law.

ISBN: 9780578744308

Imprint: Omidina Productions

INTRODUCTION TO ORISHA: THE BLACK GODS

Have you ever wondered who the gods of Africa are? In a place called Yorubaland, the African gods are called Orishas.

The Orishas represent the many superpowers we have deep inside of us. When we devote ourselves to Orisha, we unlock the spiritual power of the Orishas (African Gods) within ourselves.

Hello, my name is Oba Ade Dayo, and I have been an Orisha devotee my entire life and I would like to introduce each of these special Orishas to you, so you can learn about the powers of the African Gods that live within you.

Are you ready to become a superhero? If you said yes, then it will require hard work!

You have to learn Orisha in order to know Orisha. And by learning Orisha, you bring Orisha (spiritual power) into your life.

Your superhero mission today:

to color each Orisha in their special colors, activating the spiritual power of Orisha in your life.

- Oba

ELEGBA / ELEGGUA

"The master of the door"

Every morning before we leave the house, Elegba asks that we wipe our feet at the door so that he can keep all our blessings in the house.

And after a long day of playing outside, we wipe our feet outside the door before entering the house, leaving the ups and downs of the day outside, to come home to our blessings.

Color Orisha Elegba in his special Colors:

Red & Black

Help Elegba find his herbs and soap, so he can get cleaned up before going outside to play.

OGUN

"The role model for Intelligence"

Ogun teaches us how to be good students, so we can one day become great professionals.

Professionals have tools, knowledge, plans, actions and the ability to solve problems.

It is Ogun that teaches us how to use our tools, so that we can make plans to become great professionals.

Color Orisha Ogun is his special colors:

Red, Black, Green and Purple

OCHOSSI

"The Hunter and the Law"

Ochossi teaches us about consequences. That if we are to break the law, the law will discipline us.

Ochossi is about following directions, because the arrow follows the direction that we point it.

So let's stay on the right side of the law, so Ochossi will never have to hunt us.

Color Orisha Ochossi is his special colors:

Blue and Yellow

ERINLE AND ABATA

"The Doctor and the Nurse"

Erinle is the doctor and Abata is the nurse.

The doctor looks scary, doesn't talk much, but knows how and where we are hurt. The doctor also knows what is best for us, so we trust the doctor and the nurse to help us feel better.

The doctor talks to our body so that our body parts can tell the doctor where we are hurt. And just like the story of the frog who became a prince, our doctor will turn into our prince when we feel better.

So don't be afraid of the doctor!

Color Orisha Erinle and Abata in their special colors:

Blue, Green and Gold

BABALUAYE

"The essential worker"

Babaluaye is our essential worker in great times of sickness. Sadly in these times, sometimes people pass away.

It is Babaluaye's job to make sure that the people who pass away are taken care of, and also to make sure that the sickness does not pass onto others.

So in times like Covid-19, we thank Babaluaye for protecting our essential workers.

Color Orisha Babaluaye in his special colors:

Brown, Black, Blue and Red

ORISHA OKO, DADA, KORIN KOTO AND OGE

"The farmer, the vegetables, the Scarecrow, and the Ox"

Orisha Oko teaches us how to grow our food and vegetables, and Dada means to "be good". So, when we eat our vegetables we are being good!

The scarecrow protects our vegetables so they can grow healthy and we can eat healthy.

And it is the Ox who helps with his strength to plow the earth to give us good harvest.

Color Orisha Oko, Dada, Korin Koyo and Oge in their special colors:

Red, White, Blue and Pink

Help Jutia find the Obi so he can talk to Elegba.

IBEJI

"The Miraculous Twins"

The Ibeji's are the Orishas of twins, identical twins and fraternal twins, as well as the Orisha of opposites. And it is said that the Ibeji are really one soul that is so big, that they could only fit into two containers.

Our story starts off in a dangerous time of great fear and pandemic when Iku - (Death), was going from town to town eating everyone.

When the Ibeji heard that Iku was coming to their town Ondo, they decided to play a trick.

Taiwo, the female twin, put on some of her brother Kehinde's clothes so she looked like a boy, while Kehinde grabbed his drum. And the two set out on the road leading to their town.

They came to a crossroads and stopped by a large bush as Iku came down the road from the left as expected. When he saw Kehinde standing outside with his drum, Iku asked *"are you here to stop me from coming to your town to eat?"*. Kehinde replied, "Why yes."

Iku responded, *"well then, in what test do you dare to challenge me?"*

Kehinde responded *"I will play my drum and you will dance. The first to give up, will be the loser."*

Iku, being proud, accepted the challenge, and Kehinde began to play his drum. As Iku danced, the sun and the moon came and went, while secretly Taiwo waited in the bush. When Iku turned his head, Taiwo and Kehinde switched places, so that while Taiwo drummed, Kehinde rested as Iku continued to dance.

After 7 days and 7 nights, Iku was convinced he would tire and starve himself to death if he continued to keep on dancing. So he decided to give up and move along to the next town.

Happily, Kehinde asked Iku *"Do you give up?"*

Iku replied *"I do. You are one of Olodumare's greatest drummers."*

The challenge was settled and Iku promised Kehinde that when it was time for him to come back to collect the twins, he would always leave one behind. And so twins are known to deceive death because very rarely do twins die together.

Color the Ibeji's in opposite colors, or color them the same to trick death.

AGAYU

"The Master of Pressure"

Sometimes when we are angry, we can lose our temper and explode like a volcano.

Agayu teaches us to take a deep breath so we don't destroy the things that we love, like our toys, bedrooms and friendships, in a temper tantrum.

When the volcano erupts, we hope and pray that no one is around to get hurt.

If you are feeling upset, it is best to ask Mommy, Daddy, or the adult in charge if you can go outside to scream and let your angry voice out, instead of having a tantrum and hurting the people and things you love.

Color Orisha Agayu in his special colors:

Brown, Burgundy, Orange and in 9 colors of the rainbow.

CHANGO

"The King of Life"

Chango teaches us not to be lazy.

If we want something in life, we have to work hard to get it.

Chango also defends others against bullies, loves music, dance, and having a good time.

He is the life of the party, but Chango also teaches us to take care of our responsibilities and chores.

It is ok to party, celebrate and have fun, but only after work and study.

Color Orisha Chango in his special colors:

Red and White

OLOFI, OBATALA AND ODUDUWA

"God and his right and left hand"

Obatala and Oduduwa are the Creators of the world.

They teach us that we must work together to accomplish major tasks. No one can do it all alone, nor should anyone carry the responsibility alone.

One hand washes the other, and together they wash the face.

It is important that we wash our face and brush our teeth to honor the cooperation of the sky and the earth.

Color Olofi, Orisha Obatala and Oduduwa in their special colors:

White, Red, Blue and Yellow

Help Igbin escape from Iyo (salt).

OBA NANI AND YEWA

"The Judges of our afterlife"

When we die, Oba will write the story of our life which she will weigh against our heart.

If we have been good to people and done good deeds, Yewa will give us our wings to fly to Heaven.

Yewa teaches us that every flower represents a soul that has passed away. This is why she likes lots of flowers so she can smell their fragrance and keep away bad spirits.

Oba Nani and Yewa teach us to give our ancestors flowers to remind them of life, and to make the sad and angry spirits go away.

Color Orisha Oba Nani and Yewa in their special colors:

Pink, Orange, Burgundy and Black

OYA

"The Queen Of Masquerade"

Oya teaches us that we can be who we want to be, and that we all have different parts of ourselves.

She also teaches us how to hide from bullies.

Oya represents the ability to stand up for ourselves so that when we are afraid, we can put on a mask to get through our fear.

However, Oya also reminds us that under the mask, we are still who we are!

Color Orisha Oya in her special 9 colors of the rainbow.

YEMAYA / YEMONJA

"The Mother of the World"

Yemaya teaches us to love our mother and our grandmothers.

Mothers are always there for us, just like the ocean covering the earth, we only have ONE mother.

Yemaya is the Queen of Water.

Everytime we take a drink of water, Yemaya feeds us like how our mother feeds us.

And in the wise words of Fela Kuti

"Water has no enemy"

Yemaya teaches us to NEVER become an enemy to our mother!

Color Orisha Yemaya in her special colors:

7 shades of blue and pink (for the coral)

OSHUN

"Mother of Fresh Water"

Honey never goes bad. It always tastes sweet, and it can never be spoiled.

Oshun is the Orisha in charge of fresh water, and everyone drinks from the river.

Oshun teaches us how to get along. If we are nice to others, they should be nice to us!

But if they are not, we ignore them just like Oshun when she pretends to be deaf behind the waterfall.

Oshun teaches us how to be nice, even if we are in a bad mood, or having a bad day.

Color Orisha Oshun in her special colors:

Yellow, Gold and Orange

ORULA

"The Fortune Teller"

Orula is here to help us find our destiny.

When we come down from Heaven as a spirit we make a promise to complete a task here on Earth. But when we get here, we often forget who we are and our task.

We seek out Orula to remind us of the promises we made in Heaven and our destiny. This promise is very important to ourselves, our family and community.

When we have doubt about who we are, we seek out the Babalawo to ask Orula to remind us of the promises we made in heaven.

Color Orisha Orunmila in his special colors:

Yellow & Green

Help Agemo (chameleon), Obatala find his way to Olokun

OLOKUN

"The Owner of the Sea"

Olokun lives at the bottom of the ocean where it is deep, dark and where no people can go.

This lesson teaches us about limits and boundaries. There are places that are off limits to us, for example when our parents ask us not to go into their bedrooms. We must respect the boundaries and rules they have set for us.

Our parents bedroom is a mystery, just like the mystery of the bottom of the ocean.

There are things in our parents room that are not for children, just as there are creatures in the bottom of the ocean that people should not be disturbing.

We should respect the boundaries and limitations of our parents and elders because one day, just as the bottom of the sea will cough up precious jewels on the shores, we will become adults and understand more about privacy.

Color Orisha Olokun in her special colors:

Blues and Pink

AGEMO

"The Chameleon"

Agemo is a messenger of Orisha Obatala.

He can change into any color, and so he teaches us how to adapt to any situation.

Agemo is wise, patient and responsible.

Color Agemo is his special colors:

ANY color

AGBO

"The Ram"

Agbo was known to be the best friend of Oya.

One day, while listening to gossip, Agbo overheard that his best friend Oya was in trouble with Olofi. And behind Oya's back, he made a promise to Olofi that he would bring Oya to Olofi's house for punishment.

However, when Olofi heard Agbo's willingness to have Oya punished, he asked Agbo if he and Oya were still friends, and he answered *"Well Baba, that is why it will be easy for me to trick Oya to come to you…"*

Olofi thought for a second and told Agbo that if he didn't make good on his promise to bring Oya to him, he would hold him responsible and punish him. Agbo agreed thinking he would receive a treat or reward for betraying his friend, and as he left Olofi's office, Olofi facetime'd Oya, telling her not to open the door for anyone.

Oya confused, responded by telling Olofi that she had things to do. But Olofi went on to warn her that someone was coming to betray her. And just then, her best friend Agbo knocked on her door.

Olofi gave Oya one final instruction: to tell Agbo she was unable to have company, and to put on her 9 bracelets. That if she found herself in trouble, she was to pray to Olofi and he would help her. But because Agbo was her best friend, she trusted him and opened the door thinking he was coming to save her.

When Oya opened her door, Agbo grabbed her and put her in a box. He then dragged the box to Olofi's house. Now upset and hurt, Oya began to pray. And just then Olofi sent a great wind so strong that it knocked the box out of Agbo's hands and into the bushes allowing Oya to escape, leaving her bracelets behind.

Oya hid in the bushes as Agbo grabbed the box and shook it, hearing the bracelets clanging about in the box. *"Ah ha"* he said… *"I still have her!"*. But little did he know, Oya had slipped out the box.

When Agbo finally got to Olofi's house, Olofi reminded him of the promise he made. And that there would be punishment if he did not deliver Oya. Agbo turned the box over to Olofi, and Olofi's helpers opened the box, but Oya was nowhere to be found.

Immediately, Agbo was sentenced for punishment: he was put in time out to receive a spanking for betraying his best friend, and for lying to Olofi.

The story of the ram teaches us to be loyal to our friends, but when our parents tell us to be careful about certain friends, we must listen.

Color Agbo is his special colors:

White, Brown & Black

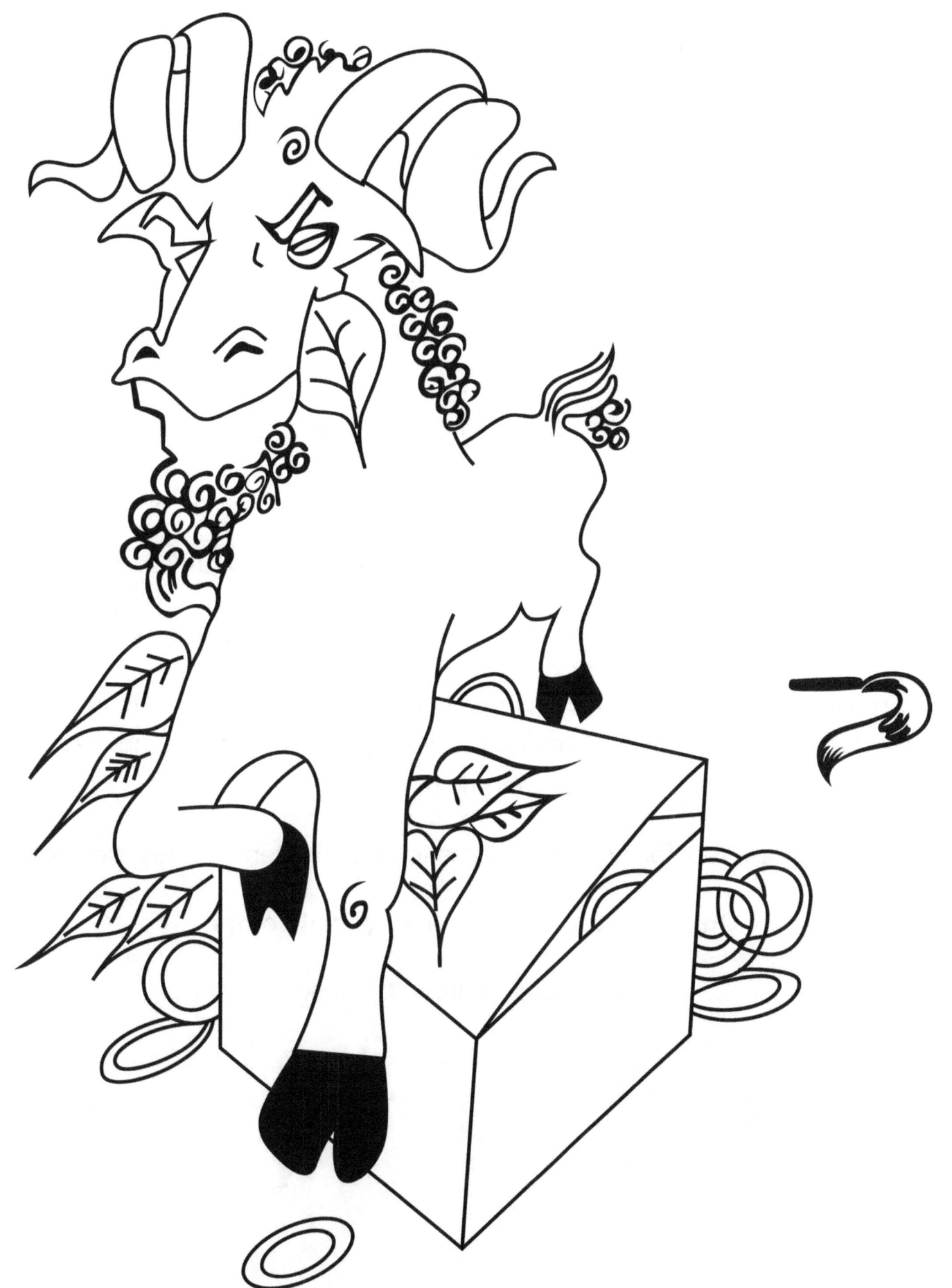

AKUKO

"The Rooster"

The rooster is Olofi's trumpeter.

In the morning, he announces the rising of Olofi, the sun.

Akuko also represents Osun, the companion of Elegba, Ogun and Ochossi.

It is his job to stand guard to protect our souls.

The rooster is the preferred meal of most of the Orishas because he is strong, honorable and responsible. And he never forgets to play his trumpet every morning.

It is Akuko, the rooster, who teaches us to be consistent and responsible.

Color Orisha Akuko in his special colors:

Red, Blue, Yellow & Black

EKU / JUTIA

"The Master of Escape"

Jutia is the bush rat that teaches us to never give up.

Although he is small, he is strong, and teaches us to push ahead when trying to achieve our goals.

He also teaches us how to always find our way home.

Jutia is the messenger of Elegba and Ogun

Color Orisha Eku/Jutia in his special colors:

Brown and Black

ELEGBA
"Elegba and Obi"

Elegba is referred to as the beginning and the end, as all things start and end with Elegba.

Here he sits on a coconut to show us that as long as we can use the coconut, we begin and end all ceremonies making sure we are right with the gods.

The story of Obi (the coconut) is that he was in charge of communicating with Olofi. But he became very proud, and one day while having a party, the Osogbo's (Iku: Death, Ano: Sickness, Ofo: loss, Eyo: tragedy and Araye: confusion) knocked on his door to join the celebration. But Obi being prideful and arrogant, refused the Osogbo's, calling them "filthy" and told them they had no business being at his party.

Elegba on his way to the party, saw the Osogbo's standing on the corner of Obi's street and asked why they were not at the party. They told Elegba how Obi treated them, how Obi called them "filthy" and kicked them out of his party. Elegba in his wisdom decided to go back and report this to Olofi

Elegba told Olofi how Obi had become rude to his brothers, and Olofi went back with Elegba to Obi's party. But before going in, Olofi asked to use one of the Osogbos coats to wear as a disguise. Olofi then knocked on Obi's door.

When Obi answered the door, he was rude, telling Olofi *"get out! no dirty people allowed at my party!"* Olofi then took off his disguise, blinding Obi with his rays of light. Obi shocked, and realizing it was Olofi, immediately got down on the floor to ask for forgiveness.

Olofi already upset, told Obi he was too prideful. He told Obi he would wear the dirty coat from now on, so no one would know the white goodness within him. He also cursed Obi that he would forever roll on the floor.

And so this is why the coconut is white on the inside, brown on the outside, and thrown on the floor. Because once the coconut was high in the tree, but then he fell from grace to the ground.

This is how Obi learned, he was never above anyone else.

Color Elegba in his special colors:

Red, Black and Grey

IYAWO

The Yawo is the newly made Orisha member of the Ile (spiritual house).

The Yawo wears all white for one year and seven days.

After one year and seven days, the yawo gets to dress in regular clothes again.

Which Orisha do you think is the Yawo's Guardian Angel? (Orisha)

Color this Yawo in the colors of her Orisha (Guardian Angel)

About The Author

Oba Olff (Oba Ade Dayo) is a 3rd generation African American Priest, Palero and Omo Ana in the Yoruba influence Lucumi Spiritual System of Cuba. With origins stemming from an African Amercian Ocha house in New York City, he travels perfecting his craft as a spiritualist and mystic. He is established as an Oriate in the United States and Cuba, where he continues to advance the practices amongst new initiates and elders worldwide. His personal mission involves the teachings of basic and foundational principles of Spiritualism, to aid the Ancestral veneration of descendants of the diaspora worldwide.

The "Kere Kere Ya" Orisha Coloring book is inspired by the memory of Omidina, Oba Ade Dayo's mother, and the visionary behind Omidina Productions.

In the 1980's Carol Ann Robinson (Omidina), was inspired by her thespian background to create **The Apataki Theater Company**, for children born into Orisha Traditions. Every Saturday for 2 years, she gathered the children in her community to teach them the folk stories, dances and songs of the Orisha, as well as the dynamics of theatre.

After her passing in 2002, her son Oba Ade Dayo committed to keeping her memory and vision alive.

May this coloring book spark the interest in Orisha folklore and empower our young black children, all over the world.

www.Omidina.com

Book. Content. Culture.